I0756248

FINISHING LINE PRESS
www.finishinglinepress.com

WHAT WE KEEP WITHIN THE LIVING

poems by

Julie Taylor

Finishing Line Press
Georgetown, Kentucky

WHAT WE KEEP WITHIN THE LIVING

for Steve

ISBN 979-8-88838-287-5 First Edition

ACKNOWLEDGMENTS

"Wildfire" appeared in *Nimrod International Journal* Fall/Winter 2013

Many thanks to Fran Quinn and over 12 years of the Chicago Poetry Workshop, to the beginnings at Britte's and the back-alley entrance to monthly zooming and to what has become vital to my life. Huge thanks to the Chicago Poetry Workshop, especially to Terry Cahill and Alison Granucci for editing help. A long overdue thank you to Mark Vinz and the late Thomas McGrath. Finally, to my family, Theo Gillie and Rob Gillie, thank you and my love, as always.

Publisher: Leah Huete de Maines
Editor: Christen Kincaid
Cover Art: Julie Taylor
Inside Art: Julie Taylor
Author Photo: Julie Taylor
Cover Design: Elizabeth Maines McCleavy

Order online: www.finishinglinepress.com
also available on amazon.com

Author inquiries and mail orders:
Finishing Line Press
PO Box 1626
Georgetown, Kentucky 40324
USA

Table of Contents

WITHIN THE LIVING

Remembering Roses

My birth
rose is *Starfire*,

that first rose I smelled
then cupped and crushed
into obliteration with my two hands

Your rose survives
fire—
that undeniable red rose
on your right shoulder

all petals on
on your dead body.

I have found a rose garden to watch
how ants decorate the dead—

Motionless honeybees
swim in lifeless petals.

December Morning

Day begins before we do,
an entire flock of hours
have already grazed the open fields
and have joined the week's migration
towards month. December
and the embers of us swept up in sleep
alight yesterday's coals—

We worship here
under the covers, the curtains closed
a naked calf, idle breasts
loins, legs and limbs—
Let us linger here, while the sun
omnipotent, celestial, indivisible
from us, can do nothing, but burn.

Aguamiel

Stored secretly in my marrow
is enough honey water
to tide me through to my life's end

more than enough
to make tequila for a city of drunks.

Half a century in, there's no doubt
the stem starting to bloom
will ruin me.

I'll keep my heart
broken, my water
what?—

for a flower.
A far more desirable drink, that
one blossom, opening—

Watercolor

New Year's Day, Mexico City

This city is splashed with heroes
I've never heard of, brushed
with Marias and mixed with martyrs,

while azaleas and poinsettias dot the littered pavements,
their bold and daring magentas are stroked
by a skillful painter to distract my eyes—

and so too the emerald leafed rubber trees
that make me look up as a young girl
holds out a bouquet of violets for a peso,

and later, when you kiss my neck,
I flush crimson red, so soaked and absorbed
into this city I am wet and washing into heaven.

Hymn

It's simple what the hummingbird wants.
What he has is a slender, slightly bent beak,
and he will go from fuchsia to fuchsia
into the petunias in search of the one unemptied cup
using each inch of his iridescent body
his nearly invisible wings
his ruby throat pulsing like blood
to drink every drop a flower can hold.

The hummingbird has no song as he dips
in hollyhocks and honeysuckles
and yet the wings on his body sing.
He hovers through trumpet trees
where angel-like flowers open so wide
petals hold him whole wings still beating.

It takes a tiny bird to hear what rings
inside the coral bells and ceaseless
meandering into all the magnolias,
to understand this whole glorious morning
before the morning glories open.

Photograph of Peaches

These two   peaches in a bowl—
how close they are   skin to skin
where even their shadows   touch another
hidden depth   of darkness.

We know   the burnt orange color
that inherits the fruit   but in this
black and white photograph   only the softness
of skin is apparent.   Inside
are the blood red parts   nearest the pit   and juice
rising to sweetness held entirely   within that skin.

What morning have we not   awoken as such, my love,
to the sunrise ripening us   to light falling around us like mercury
into the earthly creases between   our two bodies.

Unguided Tour

Memorial Day, St. Lucia

There is no one here to tell us
that the plant growing in the rain forest
is shadow bennie, that 'blessed herb'
or that the leaves, when brewed
can take away incredible pain.

We guide ourselves.
Sometimes I tell you
where to touch, or how

and sometimes you surprise me
curling a strand of my hair, your hand
following the nape of my neck
to where I can reach into the underworld
and savor a forbidden fruit.

There is no one to tell us where
the cinnamon trees grow, we are guided only
by a familiar scent, falling with the rain.

New Moon

What could the moon be up to tonight?
With its thin sliver of a beggar's cup—
fill me, I am hungry, will work for moonbeams
don't mind the mess of stars

love here and *here* and again
until both our eternities are snuffed—
the moon like a cup will go on begging again,

not all givers give enough,
you, on the other hand, know the blacksmith
the metal and the cup and what
the moon holds on to as it rises up.

The Open Marsh

in memory of Steve Warrington, 1958-2010

Marsh marigolds   hold their petals
as if they will   never open
in a marsh   that may or may not be
a body   of water when the rains fail.

His hand   went into mine
careful as a heron   stepping between flower
and leaf   into the marsh
into the dark mud to where   the root grows.

His hand was steady   in mine
as the heron stands   ready with flight
knee deep   in the marigolds
their gold blooms   bursting one by one

as if what they hold is   good enough
for the sun   and the sky where a damselfly
meets her mate   his blue body tight to hers
hovering with her above a sea   of suns.

Together they all   but disappear
as he has. Let the world   hold this
this root to flower   unfolding.

Within the Living

What will survive of us is love. —*Philip Larkin*

my earth born heart
          the sun   Morning—

another's
          only a sliver
a silver rib of moon—

          light   the dark

just shadows
          of us   just spinning
into the waning moon

          glimmering in   the dead
still   evening   waters
where stars   walk before   flying on water

Bone   my bones
          cage to my   earthly heart
this glowing ember   of sun—

          light   within the living
yes   with you I love
                                                  the stars!

WHAT WE KEEP

While You Were on Walkabout

I laughed yesterday   when I told my friend Janice
about this title   for a book of poetry, and later
we both laughed   in the front entry by the key chest,
a broken bowl in front of us. I said,   you could glue it

and she said, I   kinda like it that way, it's
life   isn't it? I stared at the disarray—
a brown shard curled into a fallen   burnt leaf
next to the most dazzling   autumn-colored piece.

They looked so lovely together,
fallen effortlessly apart   in the sunlight.

Show and Tell

I remember the   double dare look
that my mother explained   to me as
          he just   likes you.

Kindergarten   and I can still smell the sulfur
from the match he lit   right in front of me
          the cloud billowing   pick and choose

show and tell   I ran through the entire house
through whole closets   for the one agonizing item
          that might define me   sometimes

the paper bag I was given   I filled to the gills—
a bird's nest, an old stuffed brown bear, a round   rock
pictures of Harmon Killebrew   lifted from the doors of my armoire
and a letter with ideas about recycling   to President Nixon.

But that day before   World War II history classes
before   the history of film, before I learned
          knapsacks   don't hold a lot

I had to tell the first Steve I met   to please
          blow the flame out.

How to Start a Fire

In an hour   you will have eaten
your last meal   eleven years ago,
having returned   *Schindler's List*
to the resort's   movie library.
It will be the first night   in years
you haven't watched   a movie.

In the hallway   handwritten on a watercolor
are the words   "the journey is the destination."

In that   one room wooden shack
your journey   ended
"peacefully,"   I was told, "as if he fell asleep."

You had roast beef   and mashed potatoes for dinner
gave   a generous tip
otherwise   kept to yourself, the waitress said.

In an hour   eleven years ago
the witch lives   after the children
rise   they are baked.

I eat curry   curry so hot
I have to take   my clothes off.
Later I'll rememorize   the jagged shape
of the key   to something
(I will never know)   you owned.

I'll open the   wilderness survival book
that you left   in the trunk of your car,
find perhaps the   last page   you read.

Today   the page is
how to start a fire   without a match.

By now   naked as I am
I need   a fire
I'll put on   the blues
make a   teepee of sticks.

Tonight, there's no need   to light the candle
you are still   the flame.

Wildfire

He started the fire, but no flames took hold.
Heat ate all the oxygen that last night
of his month-long disappearance.

Had I found him then,
opening the door to the cabin
would have caused an explosion,
could have killed someone.

Opening the door, days after he died,
soot stirred and settled again.

Bananas were baked on the counter,
too black for bread, everything
was melted off the walls.

No time visible on the clock,
La Persistencia de la Memoria destroyed.

He started the fire *here*,
with his lips on mine,
blowing air in me as if through an oboe reed.
He blew so much air into me

flames took hold, he pounded my chest
as if it were a timpani and awoke a burning field,
my Norwegian grandmothers chanting,

å spise, drikke på ditt ord.
Oh, he ate and drank me
like that field on fire.

The neighbors running with buckets,
with wet rags, anything to contain it.

Nothing contains me now,
untying these tight knots
on the bags from the funeral home,
stretching out my soot covered hands.

Oh, this burning field expands
the picture, goes past the frame,

is frameless. This field of flames
burns our lying down together and rising up,
burns the house, the barn, the cattle,

burns these words and this song,
the rooster crowing another dawn.

Ditch

Along the roads   ambrosia flourishes
as their tender roots   crawl out from the ditch.
Growing   without tending
is what this pungent plant   knows best.

Occasionally   neighbors toss
a few black-eyed susans   to the wind
or a fire   runs through
scattering the banks   with fireweed.
"Grow here," the fire said
and their purple   heads nod.

All that grows   by the wayside
falls to the ground   and rots by spring.
Dying   without lips or limbs
hearts beating   or a single sung hymn.

Harvest Hymn

*

Outside the oldest church in Ontario,
he stands in front of two stone wings
that have sprouted and spread out
from the shoulders of a woman.
I laugh out loud and ask,
How can you not believe in angels?

*

In the cross-section of that moment
is an acre of alfalfa
rolled up tight and stuck
like a wheel in the field.

*

At the funeral home,
I must choose an urn for his ashes.
I hold and open
each square wooden box—
oak, maple, birch, ash.

*

His eyes won't open,
his eyelids are glued
and the blue alfalfa flowers
of his irises have vanished.

*

The bank has his house,
the last of his company sold.
The dishes that were his
break, one by one.

*

This field is freshly cut. A scent
so strong, there is
no forgiving or forgetting angels.

*

A combine worked this furrowed field,
cut stalks stand straight up
as if from their roots—
whole flocks, have taken flight.

JTAYLOR

Puzzle

All these hours
putting together the blue sky

and connecting the river water
with a thin slip of bridge between

only to find
a piece missing

the one

smack dab in the middle
that completes the sky

and gives the bridge
that last inch

that sparks the water
in the river to flow

Kawishiwi Falls
Ely, Minnesota

Shh, go lie down   the falling water says to you
or rather, the river says   hushed then hewn.

The vow of one day more flows   in unspoken light
through a river full   of abandoned beaver homes.

There are houses   we will never live in.
We stand in a field too far   to hear water falling.

This body of water is not   red from blood
but from the   iron rich stone.

Shh, go lie down   go to where the tamaracks
give their shadows   to the evening light.

There is the smell   of fresh cut alfalfa
there   where the doe stands and the newborn fawn kneels

no breath yet   in her bones   upright for the first time
before us   and the dark belly
of the woods into to which   she will flee.

What We Keep

I keep the sculpture of a man peering
peeling through a woman's organs
nose first in the dining room of my mind.
A gift from husband to wife.
The wife used the torso on every visitor
for a reaction exposing their character
until her eyes failed her
and the torso became an intruder.

I keep a fire burning
because a man made the fire.
I carry armloads of twigs
and broken branches whispering
love, *this word*
never burns to ash never leaves
by rising into the clouds into
someone else's heart, for I have
a letter from England in his hand
peeling each layer of my clothing off
peering, not just at my nakedness
but the universe that created my spine
still standing now, still trembling
with a rush of blood my bones, even
exposed oh yeah, I saved that letter.
I still get hot even thinking
of the first coming, the first read
my…

Love, you know where
all my birds nest
you know what to feed me
and the food left in your freezer
thawed out so I can cook the curry
remember the smell of your skin
three times more, forgive me I should share
I am so selfish, or, am I?
I love me you've said *who do you love?*

All these wildfires are waking up lovers, everywhere
to pack their things, small knapsacks with clips of newborn hair
dried roses and gold crowns—

this fire will burn everything,
but never can flames take
this beautiful oak table I've worked on
with my grandfather and his father my grandmother and her mother,
even though, "everywhere we looked was burning"
look at what burns
all the organs inside of me blood red burning.

Go ahead fan the flames wood burns the body burns,
this matchstick between my two fingers the cinnamon trees
already disappearing in the rain forest the ibis flying into the sun
the table that was set with no dishes no food no
heavenly body now, love all the world feeding me—

Last of the Honey

Sealed   in a ball jar
in the back cupboard of the house   unopened.

Honey.   Golden as the sun setting
sleeps loosely dreaming   inside the glass.

The last   of the honey, I'm told.

All the hives   are moving on.
Rogue swarms are swirling   into other dimensions.

Some suggest   following the swarms
(they'll soon have a quorum,
scout out another home
some sticky dream of a new hope).

Honeybees swarm   for survival
but they   won't move
unless that   one bee

dances   spectacularly—

She is   persistent
and the honeybees   are excited

I won't deny   their longing—
they have found   my mouth
it is   open

King Herod's Dream

As I walk through the museum exhibit,
familiar marble torsos stand at the entrance
and I whisper, *I remember you*
into the earless statue of Caesarea's Tyche

just as I had whispered into Steve's ear
at the funeral home. In the museum I search
the oil lamps for the one I found. I need
the light I once held, a light I know.

All the coins shine, they were so rusted
scattered in the ground they looked like dirt.
One display holds a single Roman amphora
and I gaze at the wholeness. *With all my heart,*
Steve said before he died, *with all my being.*

I collected every shard of a lamp
mapping the location where each piece
was unearthed then carefully numbered them all.
When I last held them, they were broken.

Herod has no city and there is no city in Caesarea.
Steve will never see or hold this amphora, whole or broken,
but this vessel could once again, carry water
could once again, bring us grain.

To the Dark Dance of Water
Italy, 2012

She has played   a record of Puccini
so many times, that   the soft clicks
where the needle   meets a crack
are now
          part of the song.

          She changed
her   whole life to come here
for an Italian man   who is now dead.

Puskás offers   both her hands
to the shimmering shoreline   as if
to greet a fleet of ghosts   of boats once
          anchored there.

I am
          alone   but here,
there is the sea.   There is
no sea   in Budapest.

All   along the harbor   in Anzio
sailboats are moored   loosely to the docks
their sails
          stowed away.

          She smiles
as if holding   a sliver of moon
like a pearl between   her lips.
I am alone,   but I am   two fish.

Here   no love is in vain.
She sways to the dark   dance of water
to the light   drumming of waves   upon land
like a needle
          on a record

to the silence   of the shore
          weighing anchor.

Salt Crystals

The day   is a Wednesday
early in the morning,   September.
The embers   of our evening lovemaking
fall from our shoulders,   the napes
of our necks.   The geese
already   announcing the way
the way home, or   away, or to

this memory: salt crystalizing   on our skin—
this is what   unfolds anew every year. Today
is a Wednesday.   Even the trees
seem to know this   and are preparing for thunder.
Leaves   are starting to   camouflage themselves.

There are so many   suns above me,
and sisters   stretching out
star arms, oh and Orion,   not, with a sword
but Orion, glittering, dazzling,   demystifying
how flesh and fire   are human

are   otherworldly, are—
how a Wednesday   years ago
still breathes   next to my breast like
a newborn   waiting for the milk to come
and my body   lets down, and there
are three stars now, that will not die   in me.

Trolling Hungry Lake

I remember the heartbeat

tug of the line
from here to there
where the lure was.

Then the silence.

This is what I have.
The open bow of this boat
my limbs my heart

these oars once trees
the line and the lure

this water the weight
left in my palms.

Notes

aguamiel—Spanish "honey water" sap of the agave plant

å spise drikke på ditt ord—Norwegian "we eat and drink in accordance to your word"

Kawishiwi—Ojibwe "river full of beavers' houses"

"everywhere we looked was burning"—from Emel Mathlouti's album of the same name

Julie Taylor spent her youth along the shores of Hungry Lake in northern Minnesota. She was fortunate to work with poet Thomas McGrath at Minnesota State University, Moorhead, where she received a BA in Anthropology and Creative Writing. Archaeological excavations led her on travels to Israel and Jordan. She received an MFA in Creative Writing from the University of Montana in Missoula two decades after giving birth to a son, Theophilus, in an apartment above an ice cream parlor overlooking the Clark Fork River. Currently, she lives by Lake Michigan in Chicago, Illinois and partakes in monthly Chicago Poetry Workshops offered by Fran Quinn. Her work has appeared in *Plant-Human Quarterly*, 2022, *Nimrod International Journal of Prose and Poetry* (honorable mention, Pablo Neruda Prize for Poetry), 2013, *Frazee Forum*, 2002, *What Matters—Selections from 30 Years of Literary Magazines at Moorhead State*, 1997, *Trilogy*, 1986 (Dacotah Territory, with Yahya Frederickson and Richard Schetnan), *Red Weather*, 1984-88, and *The Advocate*, 1983.

www.ingramcontent.com/pod-product-compliance
Lightning Source LLC
LaVergne TN
LVHW090540110826
845146LV00003B/1193